Fine Mess

Icolé Peyton

BookLeaf
Publishing

Presentation by *BookLeaf Publishing*

Web: www.bookleafpub.com

E-mail: info@bookleafpub.com

ISBN: 9789395756808

First edition 2022

Parallel

You're just like me
You look just like me
You act like me
You say & do the same exact things as I do
Everyone sees the same you
Why am I the only one who knows that you're
not me
Absolutely nothing like me
We both live in parallel worlds that nobody else
thinks ever exist
You took my motivation away
In some cases, you took my friends away
You're a horrifying storm that lingers inside me
You're unpleasant
You stole my joy and happiness
You're a monster
You're like a thief that likes to creep up when
not expected
You wear me like a costume
You wear my face like a mask
You took over my mind and are the master
running it
You pierce the inner-most deepest parts of me
Like a rusted jagged knife to the heart
You constantly stab me with excruciating pain
Troubled by what you only know best

You make me have thoughts that one day will
show as a reality
Scars my true body so that the whole world can
see
You make me cry on the inside every day
Every night
Why are you doing this to me?
I didn't ask you to be a part of me
I don't want you to help me
But you know what
You are me
The blood that courses through my veins
You are me
You're the monster that I try to keep inside
Locked away
Not to let loose
But I underestimate you
You're so much more powerful than you appear
to be
To what you look like
Act like
You often show yourself in front of those I love
dearly
Why are you trying to ruin my life?
I know that soon I will no longer have the
willpower to fight back
You damage me so much
That you feed yourself with my misery
Am I too weak to let you win so easily?

I already failed once
You made my tears completely dry up
My screaming is silent
You made my complaining sound delightful
However
My smile is the one that makes the most noise
The one that says it all
One day you'll have full control
I'll no longer exist in the world many people
know
But until then
Living in this parallel world with you
Is my only fight to come out alive and
undefeated

Sigh 1

Thoughts outside are different inside
My mind is going oh so crazy over my raging
pride
Taking into consideration the words I've
heard are set aside
To guide
To decide
Not to divide
But to collide
I've tried to speak my mind & not hide
The true feelings to provide to many worldwide
Supplied & amplified my brain starts to override
Occupied & terrified that I start to become
mortified
Saying what's really on my mind I'm actually
petrified
So I've decided to confide in myself and subside
To keep my thoughts satisfied by keeping them
from the outside, inside.

X

You're a map that holds so many directions
How can someone find where X marks the spot?
So many places to discover
But which path is the right path?
There's only one way that leads to finding that
special path
And that is the path to your heart
Your heart is the X
To reach your heart won't be an easy task
Once that special someone finds the X
Once someone digs through
The dirt
The hurt
The grim
The PAIN
It is safe to keep it hidden away
Only the strongest will come out on top
Only to be given to whoever is capable of
holding the key
To unlocking your delicate treasures
Unravelling your strings to explore your entire
world
To the deepest parts of your world
To the highest parts of your world
You are the map that only one is searching for

Deep Down

You know I mean something to you
You know you mean something to me
Even if it's not me
I still want you to be happy with who you have
I won't look at this as if I lost
I will look at this like a victory
I've accomplished my duties as a friend
The journey we both took
Through the highest peaks to the depths of the
sea
This journey was not easy
But we survived it
I am happy to say I enjoyed every moment of it
And as for myself
The heart was made to heal
Life goes on
You'll always hold worth to me
You'll always hold value to me
My diamonds may have been pretty beaten up
But you buffed out those scratches
I want to say thank you
Now its time for me to gather & collect the rest
of my diamonds
Put them in a bag
Tie it tight with strings of my heart

And carry on

Soundless Lullaby

A lost girl
Strong because she keeps on fighting
A world that can find noise in every part of hurt
as she starts to find peace in her silence
She refuses to speak up as she finds a sanctuary
She's scared that she's going to find peace in her
violence
She's hurt
But refuses to show it
But she doesn't need to be silent for this long.
Months pass and she's still fighting
Open up my darling
Open your eyes
To see the beauty God has provided.

Escape

The craving of serenity is essential
The need for it is evidential
The loud silence to fill the ears is incredibly
influential
Escape the mundane world to a place perfect for
us
For this immediate relief is a must
Something easily to adjust
If not both, let one go
Watching the sunset sky turn indigo
Let the gentle breeze kiss your skin
Never let outsiders in
This will be our secret
You and I are the ones to keep it

Piece by Peace

As I lay on my bed this night
I was thinking about you so strong.
I want to come and hug you tight.
I know to me you belong.
My love for you, my feelings are that strong.
And believe me when I say that they will never
go wrong.
I love you.
Just talking to you, I can never get a break.
Losing you, I will NEVER make that mistake.
You alone keep me awake.
And you alone will NEVER make my heart
ache.
Have a lovely night.
And yes do sleep tight so the bed bugs won't
bite.
Like always, I can't wait to talk to you in the
morning.
That'll NEVER get boring.
I can not WAIT till that day, I can finally get my
kisses
And that is something that I will NEVER let go.
Remember again, I LOVE YOU.
And I PRAY that one day, it'll be us TWO.
We see our feelings for each other grew.

I DON'T want anyone new.
Forever IS a long word & a lifetime meaning.
All we can do now is hold on strong & keep
dreaming.
My heart is beaming, my eyes are gleaming.
That we become the definition of FOREVER.
To ENDEAVOR.
And to never change for whoever.
For whomever.
To whatever.
To whenever.
And whichever.
Yes & let's not forget trials & tribulations.
Including the temptations.
Let's not try to feed in to the tension,
So we don't get that attention.
We'll show affection, adoration and admiration.
Don't forget to mention appreciation.
Whatever happens stays ONLY between you &
I.
Whatever happens, we'll stand by.
You're the only one in my eye.
You're the only person that I will NEVER try.
Okay let me end by saying,
I love you.
What we have is give & take.
And I'll do ANYTHING for you on my sake.
Which might be a risk I am WILLING to make.

Sigh 2

I can't escape the agony of missing you
We went from talking every day at every second
To almost not at all
Why?
Why was it so easy for all that we tried to build
went to waste just by a few words?
I know you're doing fine without me
I refuse to distract myself to get over you with
weak boys nor strong men
I know you aren't my infatuation
You are my love
Young hearts tend to change after awhile
But as you see mine heart hasn't toward you
Despite you trying your best to get rid of me
Desperately I want to tell you the truth
But no matter what I say
I know you'll stand by your decision
So I remain quiet
Remember you're not the only rotten apple in
the bunch
I am rotten too

Empathy

Empathy no longer exists within you
Despite the years you grew & stuck to her like
glue
You've pushed through
To pull through
To get through
To pursue
Only to end up overdue
All she wanted was to stick to you like a statue
However, you PURPOSELY withdrew
To act on selfish desires that cut and stained her
heart black and blue
Unfortunately, it became something she's used
to
Never was it what she wanted to get into
But you played her like a toy
Just how children do

Sigh 3

It's better to have a heart with no words than
words with no heart

Late Hours

The late hours are such dangerous times
They're dangerous because oftentimes
It's the crimes your brain puts you through
before bedtime
You stare at the empty black ceiling
Dealing with all the scenarios spilling
Even revealing the unfeeling of unfinished
healing
Thinking about the should've could've would've
thereof
The number one question WHY?
You could possibly cry
Trying to deny or even justify
Wanting to maybe fortify
Perhaps glorify
To verify your hunger to satisfy
What you're so dearly missing
Or could unconsciously be dismissing
Or simply reminiscing
Once the late hours have passed
No more being downcast
Never become desperate
To be temptation's culprit
So you've made it through another night
Hopefully you've made it out alright

Time

You're a diamond in the ruff
Which at many times
You make it VERY tough
Wanting to love you completely
Because you are the one
That completes me
Fears, insecurities & mistakes
Cloud your control
Wanting you to become mine
Is my ultimate goal
I get that you build yourself this brick wall
As a protectant from harm
But believe me when I tell you
You don't have to be alarmed
All I want from you is to show you
What I truly possess
Within me
Can't you see?
I am not this person
You've painted me to be
Trying to make this plea
All I want is to SHOW you
My love for you
Which has undoubtedly grew
To kiss you

To hold you
To squeeze you
To set you free
From your pain & distress
To address
What you need to progress
Within time
All will become a success
You're tied
I'm tired
Often I ask myself
Why do I continue to bother?
I'm taught from God's Word
That love endures ALL things
Which strengthens my heartstrings
I want nothing more
Than your reciprocated love
And what it consists of
Let me show you what I'm truly capable of
This heart that is so soft
I love you so much
So please
Come to me
Time will make us see
If we were TRULY meant to be

Dopamine

The master of disguise
Fooling the mind into thinking it's wise
To devise what you always have in mind
The lack of awareness to recognize
The lies
The cries
You commercialize
The demise you plant to advertise
You deceive people to think this new experience
is to be dignified
Using both heart and soul to brutalize
To desensitize
To scrutinize
To traumatize
As the "feel good hormone" to improvise
A facade of sweet little sorrows to forget what's
already been compromised
To minimize the damage you glamorize
You try to apologize and sympathize the deceit
you televise
Distraction is the mask you wear like a wolf
in sheep's clothing
Dopamine
I beg you not to take my love from me
As though it may appear to be

I truly do emphasize to empathize
Please do not euthanize the little bit of strength I
have to paralyze

Sigh 4

I don't think you truly understand
How deep I am into you
You pop up so frequently in my mind
That it's mostly out of the blue
You stick to my mind like glue
But who knew?
Through & through
What I feel is so incredibly true
I play old times in my mind like a preview
To review
All our times we spent together
Even our times when we withdrew
To make do
To get to
And pursue
You've always stayed on my heart like a tattoo
More like a statue
Never will I undo
Unglue
But always follow through
To live up to
Look up to
Get into
You're so sweet like drops of honeydew
Which is all true

I'm really trying to hold on tight like a screw
Even though at times you make me feel like I
had a stomach flu
However
With respect to
With regard to
Both our hearts are not of black
But of navy blue
That one day my dream will come true
Where we are both ones we chose to stick to.

You

You darken my mind
You darken my heart
You cloud my thoughts
There's never a time where just a single RAY of
light shines through
You speak your mind when I'm alone
You make yourself known when I become
overwhelmed
I can't trust you when it's only us
I can't think straight when you take hold of my
tongue
I'm so vulnerable to you
You make me afraid of you
You cause me to become something I'm not
But they don't know how strong you REALLY
are
Only I do
I know
They think you're easy to get rid of
You're not
You're sown into me
Stapled into me
Ripping you out will only cause me harm
Which I can't afford to experience
You hold me captive in plain sight

I am your prisoner
One day I will be set free
Not of my doing
But of yours
It was never about me
But of....... you

Alter Ego

My mind is my alter ego

Nobody knows what my mind is capable of
producing

The thoughts that rage back & forth from all
sections of my brain are waging a war against
one another

There will never be a defeat nor a victory with
this war

There's an enemy that lives within me

It's getting stronger every day that goes by

It makes me conjure up emotions that will be so
random which can be so hard to fight

I hide how I TRULY feel deeply within

Some can notice by the face I wear that day

I know I shouldn't but I always lie when I tell
ones "I'm fine"

I'm not a liar.. however, I don't want to burden
others with my problems so I have no choice

Existence has a purpose

Half of me wants to give up on that purpose

No longer feeling the same I once did in my life

Past incidents want to be part of the limelight
again

If I let that happen then the scars will show on
my wrists

Given that source of imaginary relief will only
make my enemy take complete control

Will I let that happen? Do I want that to happen?

All I can do is cry peacefully at night

Until I satisfy myself enough to fall asleep

Can anyone hear me?

I need help

I need you

Whomever you are

I know I'm not by myself

All I need right now is a hug

A hug so strong that I know that I can defeat my
enemy

I can't let my alter ego win and get the best of
me

If I win... hopefully, ones will be there to help
me claim my prize and see my victory

If I lose... then ones will know that I was a
failure not only to them but to myself

But for now I will keep my silence and wait to
get rescued from this mental prison

Bradycardia

Loving you is hard
So I don't blame you for always being on guard
You're trying to heal your heart that is
traumatized and scarred
Bittersweet is your honesty
Which you consciously constantly give politely
Never to show hostility but possibly modestly
Your assertion given sometimes needs to be
forgiven
Not to sound like an interrogation
But as recognition toward your disposition
About a decision you've envisioned
I used to think you were too strict
Sometimes it would cause conflict
But now I see why because when it clicked
It was solely for my benefit
Your character has a spark of contrast
Though struggling to deal with the past
You remain steadfast

Yearning

"I love you" means that I accept you for the
person that you are & don't plan on changing
you into someone else.
It means that I'm not expecting you to be perfect
& from me as well.
It means that I will love you & stand by you
even through the worst time.
It means loving you when you're in a bad mood
or too tired to do things I want to do.
It means loving you when you're down.
Not just when you're fun to be with.
"I love you" means that I know your deepest
secrets & won't judge you for them.
Asking in return that you won't judge me for
mine.
It means that I care enough to fight for what we
have.
And to love you enough to not let you go
It means thinking of you.
Dreaming of you.
Wanting & needing you constantly.
And hoping that you feel the same way for me.

Orphan

Alone in this wicked world
Empty in this grotesque world
My mind isn't even a safe place to call home
Darkness fills every inch of my being
My conscience talks to me like a master
Scratching the surface just to fall deeper into a
whirlpool of Hell
Escaping never existed with me
Deprived of what I need the most
I hunt
I search
But never finding anything to turn to
In the end of it all
Being released from the grip
Is so much better than holding on tight

Sigh 5

I tried finding God, but ended up with blood on
my hands.
And I don't know much longer I can stand
Is there anyone who can understand?
The screams are silent
But my thoughts are loud
I promised myself a vow
To never allow
My inner demon to come out
Which I already began to doubt
It wreaks havoc upon my wellbeing
Overseeing the true meaning behind the
reasoning
Why it holds me captive
To become more adaptive
To the horrors it powers is so attractive
Escaping its grip leaves me subjective
To have a different objective
On my perspective
On my downward spiral to nowhere
Of sheer terror
Living in a nightmare
That can't compare
In such desperate despair
I break free from this death chair

And full aware
As I leave this Earth
With on my face.. a blank stare...

Translucence

Your translucency allows only
a hint of light to shine through you so beautifully
Brutally, your scars pierce you so ruthlessly
Close to your endgame, you try to receive
immunity that is truthfully for your vitality
This monstrosity craves your scrutiny
Which usually uses it uselessly
So let your translucency have unity to naturally
grow within you...
Given the right opportunity.